The
WISDOM
of
JESUS

Contributing writer Anna Trimiew

Publications International, Ltd.

ISBN: 0-7853-1912-3

Anna Trimiew is a freelance writer and a former school teacher who holds a master's degree from Gordon-Conwell Theological Seminary. Her previously published work includes *Who's Who in the Bible, The Bible Almanac, The Bedside Book of Angels, Pocket Inspirations,* and *Bringing the New Testament to Life.*

Photo credits:

Cover photo: **The Crosiers.**

Archive Photos: Table of contents, 42; **The Crosiers:** 26, 65, 72; **John Foster/Masterfile:** 56; **International Stock:** Wayne Aldridge: 45; Mark Newman: 24; **MGA/Photri, Inc.:** 59, 66; Tom Firak: 54; **PhotoEdit:** Bill Bachman: 40; Erich Lessing: 58; **Z. Radovan, Jerusalem:** 21, 37, 41, 53; **SuperStock:** 4, 6, 15, 19, 28, 30, 33, 61; Christie's, London: 71; **Tony Stone Images:** 62; John Beatty: 51; Christopher Burki: 38; Lorentz Gullachsen: 22; Stephen Studd: 8; Keren Su: 13; **Unicorn Stock Photos:** Travis Evans: 69; Dennis Thompson: 10.

Art Information: page 4: "The Lord's Image" by Heinrich Hoffman; page 6: "Behold, I Stand at the Door" by Ludwig Haber; page 15: "Jesus and the Children" by Hugo Vogel; page 19: "The Resurrection" by Carl Heinrich Bloch; page 30: "The Good Shepherd" by Bernard Plockhorst; page 42 and Table of Contents: "The Agony in the Garden"; page 71: "Christ's Charge to Saint Peter" by Giuseppe Vermiglio.

Table of Contents

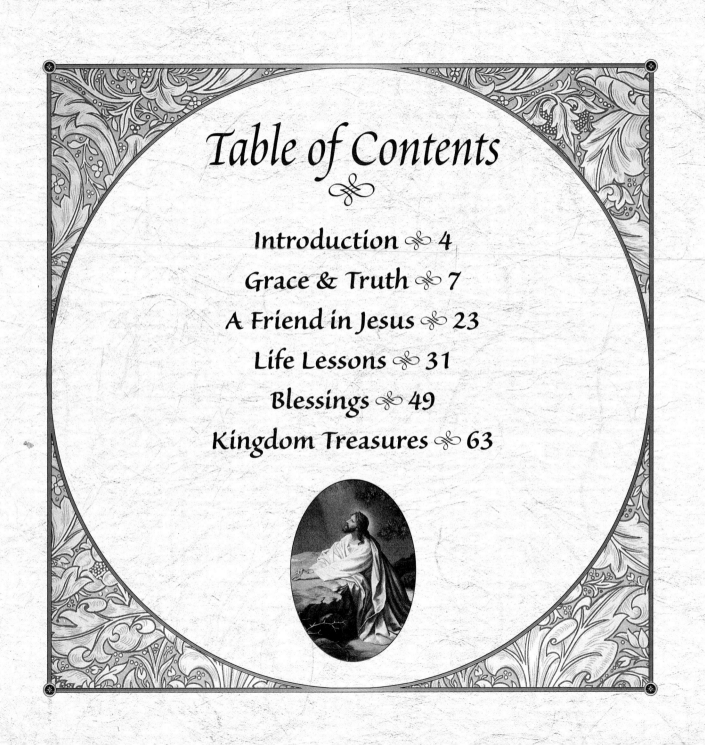

Introduction

From the moment of his birth, Jesus made a dramatic impact on his surroundings. He was born in an obscure Jewish village about 2,000 years ago. Angels appeared to announce his birth, a bright star emerged to celebrate the occasion, and shepherds hurried to his humble cradle to honor the baby's arrival. Even wise men from the East visited Judea to worship the young child.

Jesus grew up in Nazareth, and his quiet upbringing was punctuated by an important visit to the temple when he was just a boy of twelve. There, he amazed the teachers of the law by his uncanny wisdom and mature understanding of the ancient Hebrew Scriptures. Mary and Joseph were astonished by the words and actions of their precocious son, and by the unmistakable godly call upon his life.

However, Jesus did not begin his ministry in earnest until he was about 30 years of age, leaving behind his vocation as a carpenter in Nazareth. The inauguration of his life as an itinerant preacher was marked by colorful and significant events, much as his birth had been. John the Baptist announced his coming, and God opened up the heavens and poured out a blessing on his beloved son.

For the next three years, accompanied by his small band of disciples and friends, Jesus traveled from place to place preaching and healing wherever he went. Crowds thronged around him eager to hear his wise words, his surprising teachings, and his memorable stories. Still others came for healing and encouragement.

From synagogue to seashore, Jesus proclaimed the good news of the kingdom of God, turning accepted social and religious ideas upside down. He pronounced blessings on the poor, he cherished children, and he treated women with dignity and respect. Jesus denounced false religion, hypocrisy, and sin. He called for repentance, and he promised joy, freedom, and new life.

Infuriated by his growing impact, Jewish religious leaders and other detractors challenged the authority and teaching of Jesus. They arranged for his capture and death. His life, death, and resurrection marked the beginning of Christianity, which spread worldwide in remarkable fashion.

More than nineteen centuries have passed by, and his popularity and impact have only increased over time. Many give allegiance to Jesus and his teaching, regularly honoring the world's central figure on Sunday mornings in worship services everywhere. His love has transformed countless lives, and many great social causes have been fueled by his life and example.

But perhaps it is the great wisdom of Jesus that is most cherished by those who look for grace and truth in his timeless words. It is our hope that you will be blessed by his insights presented in this book and by the inspiring thoughts of others about him.

Grace & Truth

COME TO ME, all you that are weary and are carrying heavy burdens, and I will give you rest. Take my yoke upon you, and learn from me; for I am gentle and humble in heart, and you will find rest for your souls. For my yoke is easy, and my burden is light."

Matthew 11:28–30

And Christ became a human being and lived here on earth among us and was full of loving forgiveness and truth.

John 1:14, LB

I think that the purpose and cause of the Incarnation [the coming of Jesus] was that God might illuminate the world by his wisdom and excite it to the love of Himself.

Peter Abelard

And Jesus increased in wisdom and in years, and in divine and human favor.

Luke 2:52

Come, Thou Long-Expected Jesus

Come, Thou long-expected Jesus,
Born to set thy people free;
From our fears and sin release us;
Let us find our rest in thee.

Charles Wesley

… news of Him went out through all the surrounding region.
And He taught in their synagogues, being glorified by all.

Luke 4:14-15, NKJV

"For God so loved the world that he gave his only Son,
so that everyone who believes in him may not perish
but may have eternal life."

John 3:16

The Spirit of the Lord is upon me,
because he has anointed me
to bring good news to the poor.

He has sent me to proclaim
release to the captives
and recovery of sight to the blind,
to let the oppressed go free,
to proclaim the year of the Lord's favor.

Luke 4:18–19

Jesus answered, "Those who are well have no need of a physician, but those who are sick; I have come to call not the righteous but sinners to repentance."

Luke 5:31–32

"Do not be afraid."

Luke 5:10

Jesus Christ alone stands at the absolute center of humanity, the one completed harmonious man. He is the absolute and perfect truth, the highest that humanity can reach; at once its perfect image and supreme Lord.

Charles W. French

"Whoever welcomes one such child in my name welcomes me."

Matthew 18:5

Jesus said to them, "You cannot make wedding guests fast while the bridegroom is with them, can you? The days will come when the bridegroom will be taken away from them, and then they will fast in those days."

Luke 5:34–35

The Father loves the Son and has placed all things in his hands.

John 3:35

The influence of His life, His words, and His death, have, from the first, been like leaven cast into the mass of humanity.

Cunningham Geikie, *Every Knee Shall Bow*

Jesus answered, "Very truly, I tell you, no one can enter the kingdom of God without being born of water and Spirit. What is born of the flesh is flesh, and what is born of the Spirit is spirit."

John 3:5–6

How beautiful upon the
mountains
are the feet of the
messenger who
announces peace,
who brings good news,
who announces salvation,
who says to Zion, "Your
God reigns."

Isaiah 52:7

John answered, "No one can receive anything except
what has been given from heaven."

John 3:27

"The wind blows where it chooses, and you hear the sound of it, but you do not know where it comes from or where it goes. So it is with everyone who is born of the Spirit."

John 3:8

"If any want to become my followers, let them deny themselves and take up their cross and follow me."

Mark 8:34

Jesus said, "Let the little children come to me, and do not stop them; for it is to such as these that the kingdom of heaven belongs."

Matthew 19:14

"Indeed, God did not send the Son into the world to condemn the world, but in order that the world might be saved through him."

John 3:17

He called a child, whom he put among them, and said, "Truly I tell you, unless you change and become like children, you will never enter the kingdom of heaven. Whoever becomes humble like this child is the greatest in the kingdom of heaven."

Matthew 18:2–4

The people who walked in darkness have seen a great light;
those who lived in a land of deep darkness—
on them light has shined.

Isaiah 9:2

"I am the light of the world. Whoever follows me will never walk in darkness but will have the light of life."

John 8:12

"I am the way, and the truth, and the life.
No one comes to the Father except through me."

John 14:6

"Let anyone who is thirsty come to me, and let the one who believes in me drink. As the scripture has said, 'Out of the believer's heart shall flow rivers of living water.'"

John 7:37–38

And I pray that you, being rooted and established in love, may have power, together with all the saints, to grasp how wide and long and high and deep is the love of Christ, and to know this love that surpasses knowledge—that you may be filled to the measure of all the fullness of God.

Ephesians 3:17–19, NIV

This is what the Lord says…
I am the first and I am the last;
apart from me there is no God.

Isaiah 44:6, NIV

"For I have come down from heaven not to do my
will but to do the will of him who sent me."

John 6:38, NIV

Be kind and compassionate to one another, forgiving
each other, just as in Christ God forgave you.

Ephesians 4:32, NIV

It was through what the Son did that God cleared a path for
everything to come to him—all things in heaven and on
earth—for Christ's death on the cross has made peace with
God for all by his blood.

Colossians 1:20, LB

O Lord never suffer us to think that we can
stand by ourselves, and not need thee.

John Donne

The reason why Christ chose the hard way of the cross was,
among other things, that he saw beyond it.

S. J. Reid

Why do you look for the living among the dead?
He is not here; he has risen!

Luke 24:5–6, NIV

"I am the resurrection and the life. Those who believe in me,
even though they die, will live, and everyone who lives and
believes in me shall never die."

John 11:25–26

A Wonderful Savior Is Jesus My Lord

A wonderful Savior is Jesus my Lord,

A wonderful Savior to me;

He hideth my soul

In the cleft of the rock,

Where rivers of pleasure I see.

Fanny J. Crosby

Jesus Christ will be Lord of all or he will not be Lord at all.

Augustine of Hippo

"Are not two sparrows sold for a penny? Yet not one of them will fall to the ground apart from your Father. And even the hairs of your head are all counted. So do not be afraid; you are of more value than many sparrows."

Matthew 10:29–31

"All authority in heaven and on earth has been given to me.
Therefore go and make disciples of all nations, baptizing them in
the name of the Father and of the Son and of the Holy Spirit,
and teaching them to obey everything I have commanded you.
And surely I am with you always, to the very end of the age."

The Great Commission, Matthew 28:16–20, NIV

O God, we give thanks that your Son Jesus Christ, who has
shared our earthly life, has now ascended to prepare our
heavenly life. Grant that, through coming to know him by faith
on earth, we may come to know him by sight in heaven.

The Gelasian Sacramentary

"I am the bread of life. Whoever comes to me will never be
hungry, and whoever believes in me will never be thirsty."

John 6:35

"Pray then in this way:
Our Father in heaven,
hallowed be your name.
Your kingdom come.
Your will be done,
on earth as it is in heaven.
Give us this day our daily bread.
And forgive us our debts,
as we also have forgiven our debtors.
And do not bring us to the time of trial,
but deliver us from the evil one."

Matthew 6:9–13

"For the Son of Man has come to save that which was lost."

Matthew 18:11, NKJV

"If the world hates you, keep in mind that it hated me first. If you belonged to the world, it would love you as its own. As it is, you do not belong to the world, but I have chosen you out of the world. That is why the world hates you."

John 15:18–19, NIV

A Friend in Jesus

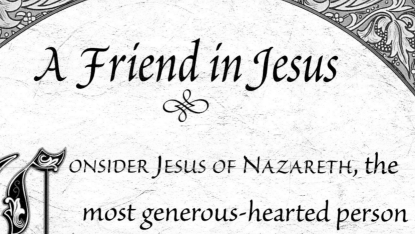

CONSIDER JESUS OF NAZARETH, the most generous-hearted person who ever lived. He never refused a request for help. Great multitudes followed Him, and He healed them all. He went out of His way to cross racial and religious barriers. He compassed the whole world in His love.

Author unknown

"I have called you friends, for everything that I learned from my Father I have made known to you."

John 15:15, NIV

"Let not your heart be troubled;
you believe in God, believe also in Me."

John 14:1, NKJV

'Tis So Sweet to Trust in Jesus

'Tis so sweet to trust in Jesus,
Just to take him at his word,
Just to rest upon his promise,
And to know "Thus saith the Lord."

Jesus, Jesus, how I trust him!
How I've proved him o'er and o'er!
Jesus, Jesus, precious Jesus!
O for grace to trust him more!

Louisa M.R. Stead

When men are animated by the love of Christ they feel united,
and the needs, sufferings and joys of others are felt as their own.

Pope John XXIII

When I met Christ at the crossroads of life, he showed me
which way to go by walking it with me.

Anonymous

I will instruct you and teach
   you the way you should go;
I will counsel you with my
   eye upon you.

Psalm 32:8

"By this everyone will know that you are my disciples,
   if you have love for one another."

John 13:35

"Whoever does the will of God is my brother
   and sister and mother."

Mark 3:35

"For my Father's will is that everyone who looks to the Son and believes in him shall have eternal life."

John 6:40, NIV

"If in my name you ask me for anything, I will do it."

John 14:14

What a Friend We Have in Jesus

What a Friend we have in Jesus,
All our sins and griefs to bear!
What a privilege to carry
Everything to God in prayer!

O what peace we often forfeit,
O what needless pain we bear,
All because we do not carry
Everything to God in prayer!

Joseph M. Scriven

"Remain in me, and I will remain in you. No branch can bear fruit by itself; it must remain in the vine. Neither can you bear fruit unless you remain in me."

John 15:4, NIV

"You are my friends if you do what I command you."

John 15:14

The older I grow in years, the more the wonder and the joy
increase when I see the power of these words of Jesus
"I have called you friends" to move the human heart.
That one word "friend" breaks down each barrier of
reserve, and we have boldness in his presence. Our hearts
go out in love to meet his love.

Charles F. Andrews

"As the Father loved Me, I also have loved you;
abide in My love."

John 15:9, NKJV

"If you obey my commands, you will remain in my love."

John 15:10, NIV

"Ask and you will receive, so that your joy will be complete."

John 16:24

Jesus Loves Me! This I Know

Jesus loves me! this I know
For the Bible tells me so;
Little ones to him belong,
They are weak but he is strong.

Anna B. Warner

"I am the good shepherd; and I know My sheep, and am known by My own. As the Father knows Me, even so I know the Father; and I lay down My life for the sheep."

John 10:14–15, NKJV

"I am the true vine, and my Father is the vinegrower. He removes every branch in me that bears no fruit. Every branch that bears fruit he prunes to make it bear more fruit."

John 15:1–2

"Go home to your friends, and tell them what great things the Lord has done for you, and how He has had compassion on you."

Mark 5:19, NKJV

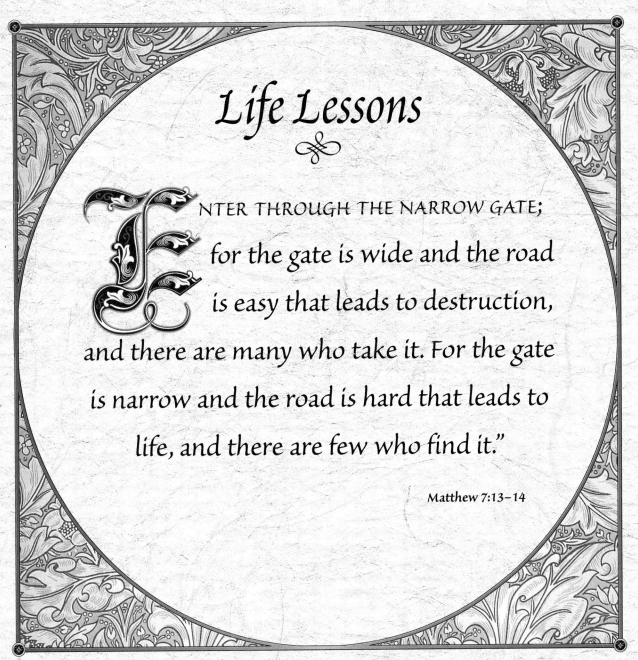

Life Lessons

ENTER THROUGH THE NARROW GATE; for the gate is wide and the road is easy that leads to destruction, and there are many who take it. For the gate is narrow and the road is hard that leads to life, and there are few who find it."

Matthew 7:13–14

"Do not think that I have come to abolish the Law or the Prophets; I have not come to abolish them but to fulfill them."

Matthew 5:17, NIV

The law indeed was given through Moses; grace and truth came through Jesus Christ.

John 1:17

"I tell you the truth, until heaven and earth disappear, not the smallest letter, not the least stroke of a pen, will by any means disappear from the Law until everything is accomplished."

Matthew 5:18, NIV

"Under the laws of Moses the rule was, 'If you murder, you must die.' But I have added to that rule, and tell you that if you are only angry, even in your own home, you are in danger of judgment!"

Matthew 5:21, LB

"Consider the lilies of the field,
how they grow; they neither
toil nor spin, yet I tell you, even
Solomon in all his glory was
not clothed like one of these."

Matthew 6:28–29

"Now you Pharisees clean the outside of the cup and
of the dish, but inside you are full of greed and wickedness.
You fools! Did not the one who made the outside make the
inside also? So give for alms those things that are within; and see,
everything will be clean for you."

Luke 11:39–41

Christ is no Moses, no exactor, no giver of laws,
but a giver of grace, a Savior; he is infinite mercy and goodness,
freely and bountifully giving to us.

Martin Luther

Teach me your way, O Lord;
lead me in a straight path.

Psalm 27:11, NIV

"If you call your friend an idiot, you are in danger of being
brought before the court. And if you curse him, you are in
danger of the fires of hell."

Matthew 5:22, LB

"If your hand causes you to sin, cut it off.
It is better for you to enter life maimed than with
two hands to go into hell, where the fire never goes out."

Mark 9:43, NIV

"So when you are offering your gift at the altar, if you remember that your brother or sister has something against you, leave your gift there before the altar and go; first be reconciled to your brother or sister, and then come and offer your gift."

Matthew 5:23–24

"And if your eye causes you to sin, pluck it out. It is better for you to enter the kingdom of God with one eye than to have two eyes and be thrown into hell."

Mark 9:47, NIV

"Don't resist violence! If you are slapped on one cheek, turn the other too. If you are ordered to court, and your shirt is taken from you, give your coat too. If the military demand that you carry their gear for a mile, carry it two. Give to those who ask, and don't turn away from those who want to borrow."

Matthew 5:39–42, LB

"Love your enemies and pray for those who persecute you."

Matthew 5:44

Lord, perfect for me what is lacking of thy gifts; of faith, help thou mine unbelief; of hope, establish my trembling hope; of love, kindle its smoking flax.

Lancelot Andrewes, *A Diary of Prayer*

"He causes his sun to rise on the evil and the good, and sends rain on the righteous and the unrighteous."

Matthew 5:45, NIV

"Be perfect, therefore, as your heavenly Father is perfect."

Matthew 5:48

"When you do a charitable deed, do not let your left hand know what your right hand is doing, that your charitable deed may be in secret; and your Father who sees in secret will Himself reward you openly."

Matthew 6:3–4, NKJV

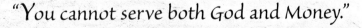

"Store up for yourselves treasures in heaven, where moth and rust do not destroy, and where thieves do not break in and steal. For where your treasure is, there your heart will be also."

Matthew 6:20–21, NIV

"You cannot serve both God and Money."

Matthew 6:24, NIV

"But seek first the kingdom of God and His righteousness,
and all these things shall be added to you."

Matthew 6:33, NKJV

"Look at the birds of the air;
they do not sow or reap or
store away in barns, and yet
your heavenly Father feeds
them. Are you not much more
valuable than they?"

Matthew 6:26, NIV

"In everything do to others as you would have them do to you;
for this is the law and the prophets."

Matthew 7:12

"No good tree bears bad fruit,
nor again does a bad tree bear good fruit;
for each tree is known by its own fruit.
Figs are not gathered from thorns,
nor are grapes picked from a bramble bush."

Luke 6:43–44

"The good person out of the good treasure of the heart
produces good, and the evil person out of the evil treasure
produces evil; for it is out of the abundance of the heart
that the mouth speaks."

Luke 6:45

"Not everyone who says to me, 'Lord, Lord,' will enter
the kingdom of heaven, but only the one who does the
will of my Father in heaven."

Matthew 7:21

"For those who want to save their life will lose it, and those who lose their life for my sake, and for the sake of the gospel, will save it. For what will it profit them to gain the whole world and forfeit their life?"

Mark 8:35–36

"Children, how hard it is to enter the kingdom of God! It is easier for a camel to go through the eye of a needle than for someone who is rich to enter the kingdom of God."

Mark 10:24–25

"And everyone who has left houses or brothers or sisters or father or mother or children or fields, for my name's sake, will receive a hundredfold, and inherit eternal life."

Matthew 19:29

"Peace I leave with you; my peace I give to you."

John 14:27

"Either make the tree good and its fruit good, or else make the tree bad and its fruit bad; for a tree is known by its fruit."

Matthew 12:33, NKJV

"Whenever you stand praying, forgive, if you have anything against anyone; so that your Father in heaven may also forgive you your trespasses."

Mark 11:25

Do not say, "I'll pay you back for this wrong!" Wait for the Lord, and he will deliver you.

Proverbs 20:22, NIV

"When you pray, go into your room, close the door and pray to your Father, who is unseen. Then your Father, who sees what is done in secret, will reward you."

Matthew 6:6, NIV

Savior, Like a Shepherd Lead Us

Savior, like a shepherd lead us,
Much we need thy tender care;
In thy pleasant pastures feed us,
For our use thy folds prepare.

Blessed Jesus, blessed Jesus,
Thou hast bought us, thine we are.
Blessed Jesus, blessed Jesus,
Thou hast bought us, thine we are.

attrib. to Dorothy A. Thrupp

"Remember, your Father knows exactly
what you need even before you ask him!"

Matthew 6:8, LB

Jesus saw the rich putting their gifts into the temple treasury. He also saw a poor widow put in two very small copper coins. "I tell you the truth," he said, "this poor widow has put in more than all the others. All these people gave their gifts out of their wealth; but she out of her poverty put in all she had to live on."

Luke 21:1–4, NIV

Now a man came up to Jesus and asked, "Teacher, what good thing must I do, to get eternal life?"… Jesus answered, "If you want to be perfect, go, sell your possessions and give to the poor, and you will have treasure in heaven. Then come, follow me." When the young man heard this, he went away sad, because he had great wealth.

Matthew 19:16,21–22, NIV

"Therefore I tell you that the kingdom of God will be taken away from you and given to a people who will produce its fruit."

Matthew 21:43, NIV

"Whoever is not with me is against me, and whoever does not gather with me scatters."

Matthew 12:30

"For out of the overflow of the heart the mouth speaks."

Matthew 12:34, NIV

"The good person brings good things out of a good treasure, and the evil person brings evil out of an evil treasure."

Matthew 12:35

"I tell you, on the day of judgement you will have to give an account for every careless word you utter; for by your words you will be justified, and by your words you will be condemned."

Matthew 12:36–37

"You have heard that it was said, 'You shall not commit adultery.' But I say to you that everyone who looks at a woman with lust has already committed adultery with her in his heart."

Matthew 5:27–28

"Let anyone among you who is without sin be the first to throw a stone at her."

John 8:7

"Go now and leave your life of sin."

John 8:11, NIV

"Do not give what is holy to dogs; and do not throw your pearls before swine, or they will trample them under foot and turn and maul you."

Matthew 7:6

"There is nothing outside a person that by going in can defile, but the things that come out are what defile.... For it is from within, from the human heart, that evil intentions come: fornication, theft, murder, adultery, avarice, wickedness, deceit, licentiousness, envy, slander, pride, folly. All these evil things come from within, and they defile a person."

— Mark 7:15,21–23

"Do not swear at all.... Let your word be 'Yes, Yes' or 'No, No'; anything more than this comes from the evil one."

Matthew 5:34,37

The divine nature is perfection; and to be nearest to the divine nature is to be nearest to perfection.

Xenophon

"Why do you look at the speck of sawdust in your brother's eye
and pay no attention to the plank in your own eye?"

Luke 6:41, NIV

"And can any of you by worrying add
a single hour to your span of life?"

Matthew 6:27

"This is my commandment, that you love one another
as I have loved you. No one has greater love than this,
to lay down one's life for one's friends."

John 15:12–13

Our Lord does not care so much for the importance of our
works as for the love with which they are done.

Teresa of Avila

Blessings

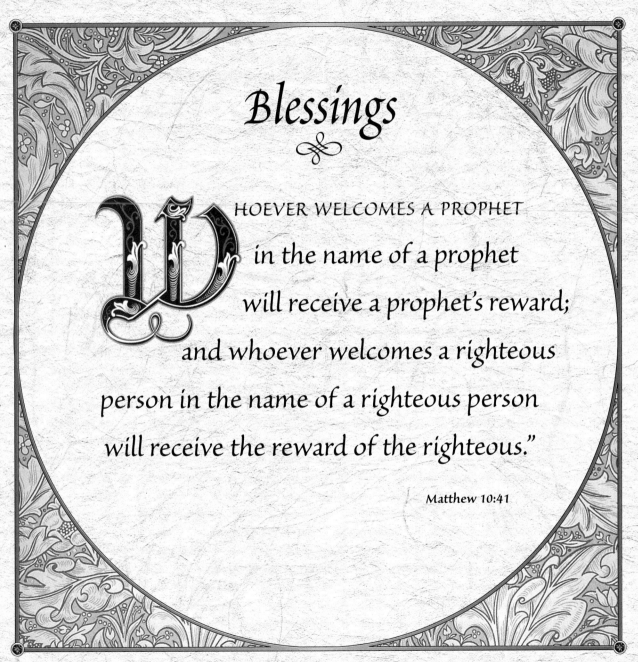

WHOEVER WELCOMES A PROPHET in the name of a prophet will receive a prophet's reward; and whoever welcomes a righteous person in the name of a righteous person will receive the reward of the righteous."

Matthew 10:41

"Blessed are the poor in spirit,
for theirs is the kingdom of heaven.

Blessed are those who mourn,
for they will be comforted.

Blessed are the meek, for they will inherit the earth.

Blessed are those who hunger and thirst for
righteousness, for they will be filled.

Blessed are the merciful, for they will receive mercy.

Blessed are the pure in heart, for they will see God.

Blessed are those who are persecuted for righteousness'
sake, for theirs is the kingdom of heaven."

Matthew 5:3–10

Jesus, Friend of the poor,

Feeder of the hungry,

Healer of the sick,

I adore Thee.

A Book of Prayers for Students

The lowly he sets on high,

and those who mourn

are lifted to safety.

Job 5:11, NIV

His miracles bore the stamp of His character.
They were not mere exhibitions of power,
but also of holiness, wisdom and love.

James Stalker, *Life of Christ*

"Take my yoke upon you, and learn from me; for I am
gentle and humble in heart, and you will find rest for your
souls. For my yoke is easy, and my burden is light."

Matthew 11:29–30

Let all the study of our heart be … to have our meditation
wholly fixed in the life and in the holy teachings of Jesus Christ:
for His teachings are of more virtue and of more … strength
than are the teachings of all Angels and Saints.

Thomas à Kempis, *The Imitation of Christ*

The King of Love My Shepherd Is

The King of love my Shepherd is,
Whose goodness fails me never;
I nothing lack if I am his
And he is mine forever.

And so through all the length of days
Your goodness fails me never;
Good Shepherd, may I sing your praise
Within your house forever. Amen.

Henry W. Baker

I will sing of the mercies of the Lord forever; With my mouth
will I make known Your faithfulness to all generations.

Psalm 89:1, NKJV

Listen, listen to me, and eat what is good,
and your soul will delight in the richest of fare.
Give ear and come to me; hear me, that your soul may live.

Isaiah 55:2-3, NIV

"It is written, 'One does not live by bread alone,
but by every word that comes from the mouth of God.'"

Matthew 4:4

Bless the Lord, O my soul;
and all that is within me,
bless his holy name.
Bless the Lord, O my soul,
and do not forget all his
benefits....

Psalm 103:1–2

"Let your light shine before others, so that they may
see your good works and give glory to your Father in heaven."

Matthew 5:16

Jesus, Teacher of patience,
Pattern of gentleness,
Prophet of the kingdom of heaven,
I adore Thee.

A Book of Prayers for Students

"...The Lord, the Lord, is my strength and my song;
he has become my salvation."
With joy you will draw water from the wells of salvation.

Isaiah 12:2–3, NIV

"But love your enemies, do good, and lend, expecting nothing in
return. Your reward will be great, and you will be children of the
Most High; for he is kind to the ungrateful and the wicked. Be
merciful, just as your Father is merciful."

Luke 6:35–36

"If any want to become my followers, let them deny
themselves and take up their cross daily and follow me.
For those who want to save their life will lose it, and those
who lose their life for my sake will save it."

Luke 9:23–24

He was very much in prayer. This had all along been His delight
and resource. In His busiest period, when He was often so tired
with the labors of the day that at the approach of evening He
was ready to fling Himself down in utter fatigue, He would
nevertheless escape away from the crowds…and spend the
whole night in lonely communion with His Father. He never
took any important step without such a night.

James Stalker, *Life of Christ*

Hear, O Lord and answer me,
for I am poor and needy.

Psalm 86:1, NIV

"Truly I tell you, there is no one who has left
house or brothers or sisters or mother or father
or children or fields, for my sake and for the sake
of the good news, who will not receive a hundredfold
now in this age—houses, brothers and sisters, mothers
and children, and fields with persecutions—and in
the age to come eternal life. But many who are first
will be last, and the last will be first."

Mark 10:29–31

Wonderful Words of Life

Christ, the blessed one, gives to all
Wonderful words of life;
Sinner heed now his loving call,
Wonderful words of life.

All so freely given,
Wooing us to heaven:
Beautiful words, wonderful words
Wonderful words of life.

Philip P. Bliss

There is no longer Jew or Greek, there is no longer slave or free, there is no longer male and female; for all of you are one in Christ Jesus.

Galatians 3:28

"For all who exalt themselves will be humbled, and those who humble themselves will be exalted."

Luke 14:11

"If you wish to enter into life, keep the commandments."

Matthew 19:17

"Blessed rather are those who hear the word of God and obey it!"

Luke 11:28

"Do not judge by appearances, but judge with right judgment."

John 7:24

"Do not work for the food that perishes, but for the food that endures for eternal life, which the Son of Man will give you. For it is on him that God the Father has set his seal."

John 6:27

Come, all you who are thirsty, come to the waters; and you who have no money, come, buy and eat!

Isaiah 55:1, NIV

He's Got the Whole World in His Hands

He's got you and me, brother, in his hands,
He's got you and me, sister, in his hands,
He's got all of us together in his hands,
He's got the whole world in his hands.

"Everyone who drinks of this water will be thirsty again, but those who drink of the water that I will give them will never be thirsty. The water that I will give will become in them a spring of water gushing up to eternal life."

John 4:13–14

Kingdom Treasures

❧

THE KINGDOM OF HEAVEN is like treasure hidden in a field. When a man found it, he hid it again, and then in his joy went and sold all he had and bought that field."

Matthew 13:44, NIV

"Therefore everyone who hears these words of mine and puts them into practice is like a wise man who built his house on the rock. The rain came down, the streams rose, and the winds blew and beat against that house; yet it did not fall, because it had its foundation on the rock."

Matthew 7:24–25, NIV

"Is a lamp brought in to be put under the bushel basket, or under the bed, and not on the lampstand? For there is nothing hidden, except to be disclosed; nor is anything secret, except to come to light. Let anyone with ears to hear listen!"

Mark 4:21–23

"Again, the kingdom of heaven is like a merchant in search of fine pearls; on finding one pearl of great value, he went and sold all that he had and bought it."

Matthew 13:45–46

"Whoever has will be given more."

Mark 4:25, NIV

"Heaven and earth will pass away,
but my words will not pass away."

Mark 13:31

Your word is a lamp to my feet
and a light to my path.

Psalm 119:105

"Again, the kingdom of heaven is like a net that was thrown
into the sea and caught fish of every kind; when it was full,
they drew it ashore, sat down, and put the good into baskets
but threw out the bad."

Matthew 13:47–49

He also said, "The kingdom of God is as if someone would scatter seed on the ground, and would sleep and rise night and day, and the seed would sprout and grow, he does not know how. The earth produces of itself, first the stalk, then the

head, then the full grain in the head. But when the grain is ripe, at once he goes in with his sickle, because the harvest has come."

Mark 4:26–29

"In my Father's house are many rooms.... I am going there to prepare a place for you. And if I go and prepare a place for you, I will come back and take you to be with me that you also may be where I am."

John 14:2–3, NIV

"If a kingdom is divided against itself, that kingdom cannot stand."

Mark 3:24, NIV

"What do you think? If a shepherd has a hundred sheep, and one of them has gone astray, does he not leave the ninety-nine on the mountains and go in search of the one that went astray? And if he finds it, truly I tell you, he rejoices over it more than over the ninety-nine that never went astray. So it is not the will of your Father in heaven that one of these little ones should be lost."

Matthew 18:12–14

"Ask, and it will be given you; search, and you will find; knock, and the door will be opened for you. For everyone who asks receives, and everyone who searches finds, and for everyone who knocks, the door will be opened."

Luke 11:9–10

"No one tears a piece from a new garment and sews it on an old garment; otherwise the new will be torn, and the piece from the new will not match the old."

Luke 5:36

"The secret of the kingdom of God has been given to you."

Mark 4:11, NIV

In God's sight a person is the most precious of all values. This truth possessed Jesus and never let Him go. He thought it, taught it, and lived it with full devotion.

Kirby Page

"For all who exalt themselves will be humbled, and those who humble themselves will be exalted."

Luke 14:11

"Or what woman having ten silver coins, if she loses one of them, does not light a lamp, sweep the house, and search carefully until she finds it? When she has found it, she calls together her friends and neighbors, saying, 'Rejoice with me, for I have found the coin that I had lost.' Just so, I tell you, there is joy in the presence of the angels of God over one sinner who repents."

Luke 15:8–10

"Take care! Be on your guard against all kinds of greed; for one's life does not consist in the abundance of possessions."

Luke 12:15–21

"Suppose one of you wants to build a tower. Will he not first sit down and estimate the cost to see if he has enough money to complete it? For if he lays the foundation and is not able to finish it, everyone who sees it will ridicule him, saying, 'This fellow began to build and was not able to finish.'"

Luke 14:28–30, NIV

"So therefore, none of you can become my disciple if you do not give up all your possessions."

Luke 14:33

"What good is salt that has lost its saltiness? Flavorless salt is fit for nothing—not even for fertilizer. It is worthless and must be thrown out. Listen well, if you would understand my meaning."

Luke 14:34–35, LB

O Lord, let me not live to be useless.

John Wesley

"Whoever can be trusted with very little
can also be trusted with much."

Luke 16:10, NIV

"The kingdom of God does not come with your careful
observation, nor will people say, 'Here it is,' or 'There it is,'
because the kingdom of God is within you."

Luke 17:20–21, NIV

To believe in Christ, I say…means
to entrust your soul to him and to
trust in him for wisdom and
strength and salvation.

Washington Gladden

"I will give you the keys of the
kingdom of heaven."

Matthew 16:19